HPS 1407

STEVE REICH

DRUMMING
PART ONE

for four pairs of tuned bongos

HENDON MUSIC

BOOSEY & HAWKES

AN IMAGEM COMPANY

DISTRIBUTED BY

HAL•LEONARD®
CORPORATION
7777 W. BLUEMOUND RD. P.O. BOX 13819 MILWAUKEE, WI 53213

www.boosey.com
www.halleonard.com

Published by Hendon Music, Inc.
a Boosey & Hawkes company
229 West 28th Street, 11th Fl.
New York NY 10001

www.boosey.com

 AN IMAGEM COMPANY

ISMN 979-0-051-21407-5

First printed 2012

Printed and distributed by Hal Leonard Corporation, Milwaukee WI

Note by the Composer

For one year, between the fall of 1970 and the fall of 1971, I worked on what turned out to be the longest piece I have ever composed. *Drumming* lasts from 55 to 75 minutes (depending on the number of repeats played) and is divided into four parts that are performed without pause. The first part is for four pairs of tuned bongo drums, stand-mounted and played with dowel sticks; the second, for three marimbas played by nine players together with two women's voices; the third, for three glockenspiels played by four players together with whistling and piccolo; and the fourth section is for all these instruments and voices combined. This is the score for *Drumming Part One*.

I am often asked what influence my visit to Africa in the summer of 1970 had on *Drumming*. The answer is confirmation. It confirmed my intuition that acoustic instruments could be used to produce music that was genuinely richer in sound than that produced with electronic instruments, as well as confirming my natural inclination towards percussion (I became a drummer at the age of 14).

Drumming begins with two drummers building up the basic rhythmic pattern of the entire piece from a single drum beat, played in a cycle of twelve beats with rests on all the other beats. Gradually additional drumbeats are substituted for rests, one at a time, until the pattern is completely built up. The reduction process is simply the reverse where rests are gradually substituted for beats, one at a time, until only a single beat remains. There is, then, only one basic rhythmic pattern for all of *Drumming*:

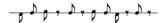

This pattern undergoes changes of pitch, phase position and timbre, but all the performers play this pattern, or some part of it, throughout the entire piece.

—Steve Reich
1971

Performance Notes

Instruments: The bongo drums are stand mounted and played with dowel sticks. One end of the stick is covered with several layers of felt, or some other padding to make the soft stick, while the uncovered wood end is the hard stick. The bongo drums are tuned and arranged for the drummers, who stand while playing, as shown below.

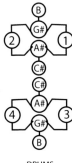

DRUMS

The above illustrates the suggested positions of the four percussionists.

Tuning the drums: The best bongo drums tend to have leather heads. This means they will have to be tuned and re-tuned to stay in correct pitch as specified in the drawing above and in the score. To accomplish this, one must re-tune the drums many times during the day of the concert. If the weather is unstable, even more tuning is required as the heads react to the moisture or dryness of the air around them. Even when the musicians walk on stage to begin the performance they should do a final tuning check and adjustment on stage. If they are recording the piece even more attention to tuning must be paid since an out of tune set of drums ruins any performance.

Amplification: One mic is placed below each of the four pairs of bongo drums. The sound engineer can set them so that all drums are equally amplified. Perhaps a slight boost for the lower frequencies will give the drums more pitch. The sound engineer should have his/her mixing desk placed in a good center location in the audience so that he/she can hear the musicians and loudspeakers very clearly, and should also be understood as a member of the performing ensemble.

In a hall with less than five hundred seats, it may be best to perform with no amplification.

About this Edition

I composed Drumming in 1970 – 1971. It was mostly jotted down in short hand in my music notebook. I would then teach members of my ensemble how to play the piece during rehearsals by playing them the patterns, showing how to phase ahead, rehearsing it, and so on. Only after the entire piece was completed did I make an ink manuscript which in many ways was difficult to read, ambiguous as to interpretation and in some cases, mistaken as to note values in the voices and piccolo parts. For 40 years, this manuscript has circulated and an increasing number of unfortunate performances have been the result.

A few years ago, I once again turned to composer Marc Mellits, who had done such an outstanding job putting *Music for 18 Musicians* into a clear, legible score form, and asked him to help me do the same with *Drumming*. This present edition is the result.

The clarifications and improvements are obvious. The score reads normally from left to right, instead of sometimes having to jump down a column of bars in the manuscript. The resulting patterns; first played by the drums at bar 21, are now all clearly written out. Prior to this, in performances during the last few years, I have heard resulting patterns played ad lib by as many as nine drummers (instead of one or two) for as long as 50 minutes (instead of about 10), other patterns were obviously worked up ad lib due to insufficient rehearsal time. Now all ensembles can play the resulting patterns as they were originally written. The flexibility of pacing that is characteristic of *Drumming* has been maintained and clarified with maximum and minimum numbers of repeats indicated over each bar. Musicians in the ensemble choose, within these limits, as to when to move on to the next bar. The overall duration can thus vary from about 16 to 20 minutes.

I want to thank Marc Mellits once again for his invaluable help in preparing this edition.

–Steve Reich
2011

Anmerkung des Komponisten

Ein Jahr lang, genauer gesagt zwischen Herbst 1970 und 1971, arbeitete ich, wie sich später herausstellen sollte, an dem längsten Stück, dass ich je komponiert habe. *Drumming* dauert zwischen 55 und 75 Minuten (je nach Anzahl der gespielten Wiederholungen). Es besteht aus vier Parts und wird "Attacca", sprich ohne Pausen, gespielt. Der erste Part ist für vier mit Stöcken gespielte und auf Ständer montierte, gestimmte Bongo-Paare geschrieben; der zweite für drei von neun Musikern gespielte Marimbas, welche von zwei Frauenstimmen begleitet werden; der dritte für drei von vier Musikern gespielte Glockenspiele sowie Lippenpfeifen und eine Piccoloflöte. Der vierte Part ist für alle zuvor aufgeführten Instrumente und Stimmen. Die vorliegende Ausgabe ist die Partitur zu *Drumming Part One*.

Ich werde oft gefragt, welchen Einfluss mein Besuch in Afrika im Sommer 1970 auf *Drumming* hatte. Die Antwort lautet *Bestätigung*. Meine Intuition wurde insofern bestätigt, dass akustische Instrumente Musik hervorbringen können, die wesentlich reichhaltiger an Klang ist als elektronische Instrumente. Als Weiteres sehe ich darin auch meine natürliche Vorliebe zu Perkussionsinstrumenten bestätigt, die sich mir bereits im Alter von 14 Jahren zeigte, als ich das Schlagzeugspielen begann.

Der Übergang von den Glockenspielen zum letzten Abschnitt des Stückes, worin alle Instrumente kombiniert werden, wird durch einen neuen musikalischen Prozess eingeleitet, den ich "build-up" (Aufbau) und "reduction" (Abnahme) nenne. *Drumming* beginnt mit zwei Perkussionisten, welche das rhythmische Grundpattern des gesamten Stückes aus einem einzigen Schlag hervorgehend aufbauen, basierend auf einer zwölfschlägigen Periode mit Pause auf den jeweils anderen Zählzeiten bis letzten Ende das vollständige Pattern "aufgebaut" ist. Allmählich hinzukommende Schläge ersetzen die Pausen Stück für Stück bis das Pattern vollständig aufgebaut ist. Der "Reduction"-Prozess hingegen stellt das Gegenteil dar; hier werden Schläge allmählich durch Pausen ersetzt bis nur noch ein einziger Schlag übrig bleibt. Demnach besteht *Drumming* aus nur einem grundlegenden rhythmischen Pattern:

Dieses Pattern unterliegt Veränderungen verschiedener Parameter wie Tonhöhe, Klangfarbe und "Changing of Phase Position" (rhythmischer Verschiebung), jedoch wird ein und dasselbe Pattern von allen Spielern das ganze Stück hindurch gespielt.

—Steve Reich
1971

Aufführungshinweise

Instrumente: Die Bongos werden auf Ständer montiert und mit "Dowel"- Sticks gespielt. Ein Ende des Schlägels ist mit mehren Filzlagen oder einem anderen weichen Material umwickelt und stellt somit den "Soft"-Stock dar, wohingegen das andere Ende, das nicht umwickelte Holz, den "Hard"-Stock darstellt. Die Bongos werden gestimmt und für die Perkussionisten wie unten abgebildet angeordnet.

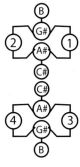

DRUMS

Die obige Darstellung zeigt die empfohlene Aufstellung der vier Perkussionisten.

Das Stimmen der Trommeln: Die besten Bongos sind generell mit Leder bespannt, das heißt sie müssen mehrmals nachgestimmt werden bis sie schließlich in gewünschter Tonhöhe bleiben, so wie es in obiger Darstellung und Partitur beschrieben ist. Um dies zu gewährleisten muss man die Trommeln am Tag der Aufführung mehrfach nachstimmen. Bei wechselndem Wetter ist das Stimmen umso wichtiger, da die Häute auf Feuchtigkeit und trockene Luft stark reagieren. Ein letztes Mal sollte die Stimmung überprüft, und wenn nötig nachgestimmt werden, sobald die Musiker auf die Bühne gehen. Hierzu sollten die Marimbas als Tonhöhenreference dienen. Sollte das Stück aufgenommen werden ist es noch weitaus wichtiger auf die Stimmung zu achten, denn ein verstimmtes Paar Trommeln ruiniert die Qualität der musikalischen Darbietung.

Mikrofonierung: Jeweils ein Mikrophon wird unter jedem der vier Bongo-Paare platziert. Der Tontechniker platziert die Mikrophone so, dass alle Trommeln gleichlaut verstärkt sind. Eventuell kann eine kleine Anhebung der tiefen Frequenzen mehr Tonhöhe verleihen. Das Mischpult sollte in der Mitte des Publikums platziert sein, so dass der Tontechniker die Musiker und Lautsprecher deutlich hört. Dieser sollte die Lautstärkeverhältnisse während der Aufführung nach Nöten ausbalancieren. Der Tontechniker ist als Teil des aufführenden Ensembles zu sehen.

Eventuell erzielt einen Nich-Mikrofonierung in einem Konzertsaal mit weniger als 500 Sitzplätzen einen besseren Klang.

Angaben zu dieser Ausgabe

Drumming komponierte ich zwischen 1970 und 1971. Die meisten Notizen hielt ich nur flüchtig in meinem Musiknotizbuch fest um die Musiker meines Ensembles während den Proben, in denen sie die Pattern spielen, zu lehren wie das Stück mit jeweils richtiger Phasenlage zu spielen ist. Erst nachdem das Stück komplett war, erstellte ich eine handgeschriebene Partiture. Diese jedoch war in vielerlei Hinsicht schwer zu lesen. Mehrdeutigkeit in Interpretation sowie in manchen Fällen missverständliche Notation der Stimmen und Piccolo Parts waren der Fall. 40 Jahre lange war es möglich diese Version der Partitur zu erhalten, woraus eine große Anzahl von "unglücklichen" Aufführungen resultierte.

Vor einigen Jahren habe ich mich einmal mehr an den Komponisten Marc Mellits gewandt, welcher die herausragende Arbeit vollbracht hat *Music for 18 Musicians* in eine klare, verständliche Notenform zu bringen, und ihn gebeten dasselbe mit *Drumming* zu tun. Die hier vorliegende Ausgabe ist das Ergebnis.

Die Klarstellungen und Verbesserungen sind offensichtlich. Die Partitur ist nun auf herkömmliche Weise von links nach rechts zu lesen, anstelle des Umstandes manchmal in der Partitur mehrere eintaktige Notensysteme nach unten springen zu müssen. Die resultierenden Pattern sind unmissverständlich notiert: Eins wird zunächst von den Trommeln in Takt 21 gespielt, ein anderes von Frauenstimmen in Takt 230 und im letzten Part in Takt 589 gesungen, und schließlich das in Takt 426 und im letzten Part in Takt 594 entweder lippenpfeifend oder mit Piccoloflöte und Glockenspiel gespielte Pattern. In Aufführungen während den letzten Jahre habe ich, dieser neuen Notation vorausgehend, resultierende Pattern von nicht weniger als neun Musiker "ad lib" gespielt (anstelle von einem oder zwei) und bis zu 50 Minuten (anstelle von 10) gehört. Auf Grund von mangelnder Probezeit wurden andere Pattern offensichtlich ad lib gespielt. Ähnliche Ergebnisse zeigten sich bei den Frauenstimmen, Lippenpfeifen und Piccoloflöte. Nun können alle Ensembles das Stück so spielen, wie es ursprünglich geschrieben wurde. Die Flexibilität des zeitlichen Ablaufes, als Charakteristik von *Drumming*, wurde erhalten und konnte durch Angabe über allen Takten von Minimum- und Maximumwiederholungen geklärt werden. Die Musiker des Ensembles wählen unter Einhaltung dieser Limits wann sie zum nächsten Takt fortschreiten wollen. Die Gesamtdauer kann somit von etwa 16 bis 20 Minuten variieren.

Ich will Marc Mellits noch einmal ganz herzlich für seine unschätzbare Hilfe bei der Erstellung dieser Ausgabe danken.

—Steve Reich
2011

Note du compositeur

J'ai travaillé pendant un an, de l'automne 1970 à l'automne 1971, à cette pièce qui s'est révélée la plus longue que j'ai jamais composée. *Drumming*, d'une durée de 55 à 75 minutes (en fonction du nombre de reprises jouées), est divisée en quatre parties enchaînées sans interruption. La première partie est destinée à quatre paires de bongos accordés, montés sur des supports et frappés avec des baguettes, la deuxième à trois marimbas joués simultanément par neuf interprètes et accompagnés de deux voix de femmes, la troisième à trois glockenspiels joués par quatre instrumentistes qui prennent aussi en charge le sifflement et le piccolo et la quatrième à l'ensemble des instruments et des voix. Cette partition est celle de la Première partie de *Drumming*.

On me pose souvent la question de l'influence que ma visite en Afrique de l'été 1970 a eue sur *Drumming*. Elle fut une confirmation de mon intuition de la capacité des instruments acoustiques de produire une musique d'une sonorité authentiquement plus riche que celle obtenue par des instruments électroniques, tout en renforçant mon inclination naturelle vers la percussion (que j'ai commencé à pratiquer dès l'âge de quatorze ans).

Drumming débute par l'installation par deux instrumentistes du motif rythmique de base de toute la pièce, à partir d'une seule pulsation de bongo, jouée au sein d'un cycle de douze battements remplacés par des silences. Peu à peu, de nouveaux battements des bongos se substituent, un par un, aux silences, jusqu'à formation intégrale du motif. Le procédé de réduction consiste, à l'inverse, à substituer, un par un, des silences aux battements jusqu'à ce que ne demeure qu'un seul battement. Il existe, donc, un seul motif rythmique de base pour l'ensemble de *Drumming* :

Ce motif subit des changements de hauteur, de position de phase et de timbre mais tous les interprètes jouent ce motif, en entier ou en partie, tout au long de la pièce.

—Steve Reich
1971

Recommandations pour l'exécution

Instruments : Les bongos seront montés sur des supports et frappés par des baguettes à double extrémités. L'une des extrémités de la baguette sera recouverte de plusieurs épaisseurs de feutre, ou d'autre textile, pour la baguette douce, tandis que l'extrémité en bois servira de baguette dure. Les bongos seront accordés et disposés selon sur le schéma ci-dessous, les instrumentistes jouant debout.

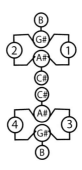

DRUMS

Ce schéma indique la position recommandée des quatre interprètes.

Accord des bongos : Les meilleurs bongos étant tendus de peau, il s'ensuit qu'ils devront être accordés et réaccordés pour garder la hauteur correcte spécifiée dans le schéma précédent et dans la partition. Pour cela, il faudra réaccorder les bongos plusieurs fois le jour du concert. En cas d'instabilité météorologique, cette opération devra être renouvelée de nombreuses fois car les peaux réagissent à l'humidité ou à la sécheresse de l'air ambiant. A leur entrée sur scène avant l'exécution, les musiciens devront procéder aux derniers accordages et ajustements sur scène. Lors d'un enregistrement, un soin encore plus grand sera porté à l'accord, des bongos mal accordés anéantissant toute l'interprétation.

Amplification : Un micro sera placé en dessous de chaque paire de bongos. L'ingénieur du son les réglera de façon que tous les bongos soient amplifiés de manière égale. La console de régie du son sera placée au milieu du public de manière à ce que l'ingénieur du son, qui est considéré comme un des interprètes de l'ensemble musical, entende très clairement les musiciens et les haut-parleurs.

Dans une salle de moins de cinq cents places, l'œuvre sera de préférence exécutée sans amplification.

Observations sur cette édition

J'ai composé *Drumming* en 1970/71 et l'avais, en grande partie, consigné en abrégé dans mon carnet d'esquisses musicales. J'exposai ensuite au cours des répétitions à chaque membre de mon ensemble comment jouer en leur interprétant les motifs, leur montrant comment les déphaser, les entraînant, etc. Ce n'est que quand la pièce fut complètement achevée que j'en notai un manuscrit, très difficile à déchiffrer par plusieurs aspects, ambigu quant à son interprétation et comportant parfois des durées fausses dans les parties des voix et du piccolo. Pendant quarante ans, ce manuscrit a circulé donnant lieu à un nombre croissant d'exécutions approximatives.

Il y a quelques années, je m'adressai, une fois de plus, au compositeur Marc Mellits qui, effectuant un travail exceptionnel, avait réalisé une partition claire et lisible de *Music for 18 Musicians* et lui demandai de m'aider à procéder à la même démarche pour *Drumming*. Cette nouvelle édition en constitue le résultat.

Les clarifications et améliorations sont évidentes. La partition se lit normalement de gauche à droite, au lieu d'avoir à sauter les mesures en colonnes du manuscrit. Les motifs, d'abord joués par les bongos à la mesure 21, sont maintenant tous nettement transcrits. De plus, J'ai entendu parfois, lors d'exécutions données au cours des dernière années, des configurations jouées *ad lib.* par un nombre d'instrumentistes allant jusqu'à neuf (au lieu d'un ou deux) pendant quelques cinquante longues minutes (au lieu d'environ dix minutes), tandis que d'autres configurations étaient à l'évidence improvisées par manque de répétitions suffisantes. Désormais, tous les ensembles peuvent jouer les configurations résultantes telles qu'elles furent écrites à l'origine. La souplesse de pulsation caractéristique de *Drumming* a été maintenue et explicitée par l'indication d'un nombre minimum et maximum de reprises au-dessus de chaque mesure. Les musiciens de l'ensemble choisissent, à l'intérieur de ces limites, le moment de passer à la mesure suivante. La durée d'ensemble de la pièce peut donc varier d'environ 16 à 20 minutes.

Je tiens à renouveler mes remerciements à Marc Mellits pour son aide inestimable dans la préparation de cette édition.

—Steve Reich
2011

World premiere on December 3, 1971
at the Museum of Modern Art, New York, NY
by Steve Reich and Musicians

Recorded by Steve Reich and Musicians on Deutsche Grammophon 474 323-2
Recorded by Steve Reich and Musicians on Nonesuch 79170
Recorded by So Percussion on Cantaloupe 20126
Recorded by Ictus Ensemble on Cypress 5608

Duration: *ca.* 20 minutes

Performance materials are available from the Boosey & Hawkes Rental Library

DRUMMING PART ONE

STEVE REICH
(1971)

Throughout the piece, the alternation of stems up and stems down
in the piece indicates the alternation of right and left hands.
The choice as to which hand is indicated by
stems up or down is left to the performers.

2

* After several seconds of getting comfortable in close unison, Drummer 2 begins to slightly increase their tempo so that after 20 or 30 or more seconds s/he has finally moved one quarter note ahead of Drummer 1, as shown at 20 . The dotted lines indicate this gradual shift in phase relation between the two drummers.

4

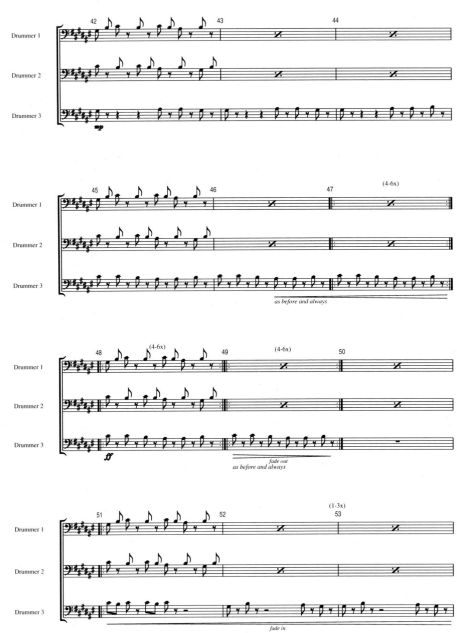

6

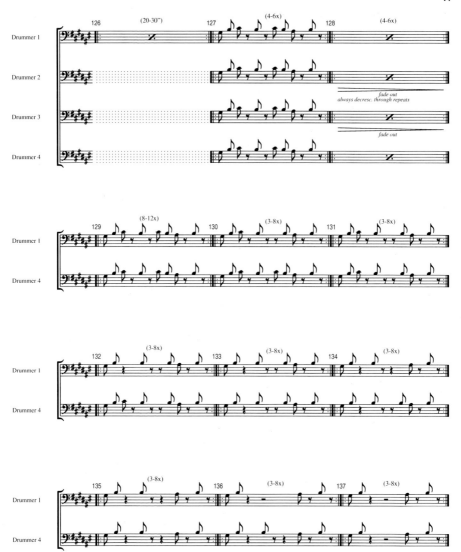

12

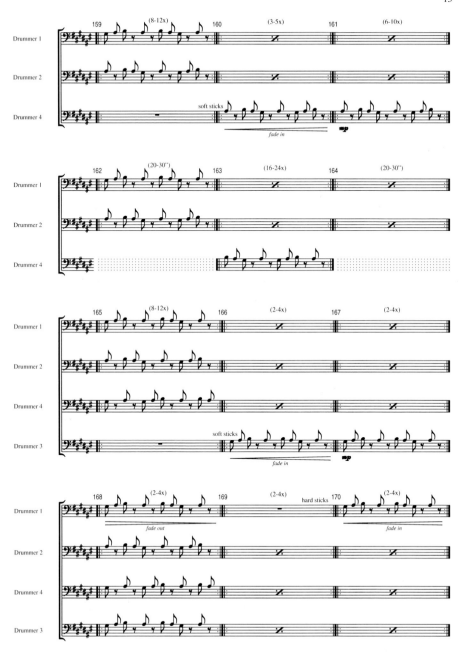

14

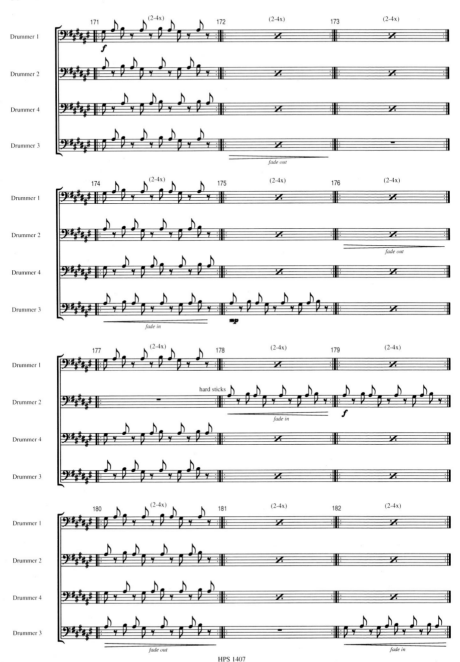

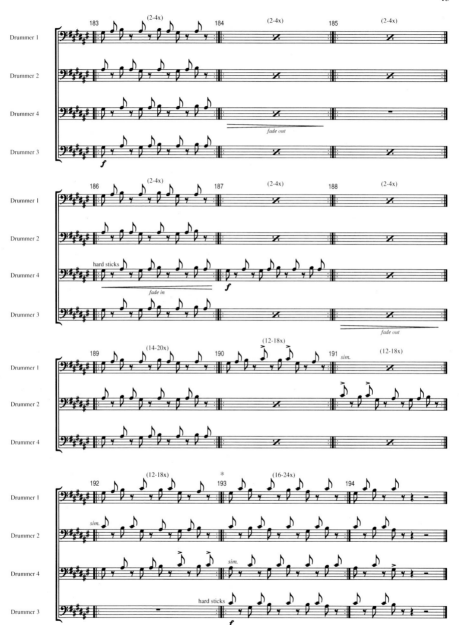

* Drummer 4 nods on the third beat of the measure, and after two repeats, all move to measure 194 together.